POCKET GUIDE TO INCREASE YOUR PERSONAL AND ORGANIZATIONAL VALUE

THOMAS C. PINNOW

ISBN 979-8-88616-396-4 (paperback)
ISBN 979-8-88616-397-1 (digital)

Christian Faith Publishing
832 Park Avenue
Meadville, PA 16335
www.christianfaithpublishing.com

Printed in the United States of America

SPECIAL ACKNOWLEDGMENT

The following people helped me complete this publication. Their professional input was extremely helpful and fine-tuned the final product. A special thank you to:

Michael Nelson
Brad and Tonya Umbarger
Christine Starr
Kim Sponem

CONTENTS

INTRODUCTION

It is safe to say that most people would like to be more valuable, appreciated and to earn more money. Yet most people are unwilling to improve their performance to do it. They show up at work, perform their basic duties, sometimes only the minimum required, and then go home. This is not a winning combination to increase your value or income.

We all experience poor customer service frequently. If you provide poor customer service, you are not going to grow your value or income, and you are not helping your employer succeed. This also is not a winning combination.

This booklet was written to help you increase your income by honing your personal skills and improve your customer service skills and *your value.* There is a catch, though. You must be willing to put forth the effort needed. Are you? It will take persistent effort. You can't just read it and expect a raise. You must earn it! Not everyone will act on these recommendations so this creates an opportunity for you to stand out. Take these recommendations seriously and act on them. Mark this booklet up, make notes, highlight what is important to you, and refer to it frequently. Ask your supervisor for their input on how you can improve. Even if you don't want to hear it, you need to if you want to improve. Set personal goals, and set goals with your supervisor.

If you are an employer, sometimes your staff may not *hear* you communicate your values and standards. For whatever reason, hearing it from an outside source has more impact. I hope this booklet will have that impact. Give every employee their own copy, or give it to people you want to improve. Set goals with them. It will work, but *you* must follow through regularly. Use it in performance reviews to improve individual performance. Use it to help set standards. It is written in outline form so you can easily communicate with someone about a specific item. Use it in team meetings for training or to address some current customer service issues. Remember, if you are a supervisor you must set an example. For instance, if you want your team to be on time, you must be on time.

I sincerely hope this publication will help you and your organization improve customer service and increase the value of your team and your organization. Godspeed.

Kind regards,
Tom Pinnow

DO YOU WANT TO BE MORE VALUABLE?

Everyone would like to make more money. But to earn more money, *you* need to improve your performance and increase your value.

Let's start by talking about what may be expected of you. It is important to fulfill your duties and responsibilities because that is why you were hired. If you don't fulfill these basic duties, you cannot expect to advance, including making more money. If you fulfill these duties well, you are a good employee and you add value to your organization, but to advance in your career and *earn* its financial rewards, you will need to perform above and beyond what is just expected of you. You need to make yourself stand out as a high performer. The goal of this booklet is to help you stand out as someone who has *earned* the opportunity to advance in your career. It is not all-inclusive, so feel free to add your own ideas about how you can progress and consider talking with your supervisor for ideas.

What may be expected of you? This is a long list, so I won't list them here. You can find the comprehensive list in appendix A. You are probably doing many of them, so don't worry. As a reminder, some of the basics are the following:

- Be honest and ethical.
- Be respectful to everyone.
- Be enthusiastic.
- Be dependable.
- Be productive.
- Be on time for everything—work, meetings, webinars, etc.
- Be helpful and friendly to everyone.
- Be good at what you do.

Most employers would be ecstatic if you are doing all on this list, and most will reward you accordingly. I wanted to make this list to give you an idea of what some employers expect from their employees. Employers with high standards may think that if you do what is listed, you may not deserve *extra* pay because you are doing what is expected of you. If this is the case, you will need to go above and beyond this list to show that you deserve extra pay and responsibility. Circle the numbers in appendix A you want to improve, and list what you will do below each one, or use appendix B to help you.

WHAT MUST HAPPEN TO INCREASE YOUR INCOME?

1. Customer service: Your organization's success depends on good customer service. Candidly, *are* you the best you can be? Are your customers happy they dealt with you?
2. Self-improvement: What are you doing to improve your value to your organization? Are you taking advantage of educational opportunities provided by your organization? Are you doing anything on your own to be the best you can be? Do you use downtime to learn more about your job and/or your organization?
3. What makes you more valuable?
    a) *Education.* Are you growing in knowledge?
    b) *Product knowledge.* Do you know your organization's products and services very well?
    c) *Know your competition.* Why is your organization better? Consider having their ads

available to help them compare and stay with you.

d) *Poise, under pressure.* How well do you handle conflict with your coworkers, supervisor, and your customers?

e) *Be upbeat and happy.* Be a "good" finder, not a fault finder. (If you truly do not like your job, it may be time to move on, *but give these tips a try.* It may change your attitude.)

f) *Communication skills*, including grammar. Do you use proper grammar in your communications?

4. Punctuality. The habit of being on time is vital. If you are chronically late, it means your supervisor must deal with it, so other employees do not follow your irresponsible lead. It is calling attention to you in a negative way. This will *not* help you.
5. Dependability. Can your coworkers and supervisor depend on you? If they cannot, you will lose their respect and diminish your value.
6. Harmony with your coworkers. It is imperative to your coworkers and your organization that the entire team works in harmony. It does not mean that you must love every coworker, but you must

set aside any negative feelings and work with them to support their role in your organization. If you do not, you will become less valuable. If you have a conflict with someone, do not let your imagination run wild. You need to talk with them in a calm, objective, and adult manner. Put yourself in their shoes when you analyze any differences. Many times, it is a simple misunderstanding. Approach them in a fact-finding frame of mind. For example, you could say, "You are important to our organization, so I want to have a good working relationship with you, but I sense we may have a misunderstanding. Have I done something you don't like? Can we talk about it?" If this approach does not resolve the conflict, then go to your supervisor.

7. What does your organization need to give you a raise? Your organization, whether it is nonprofit or for-profit, needs to make a healthy, consistent profit. This is necessary to increase your pay and

to be a viable organization. So whatever you can do to help them succeed will help *you* succeed.

- Be responsible and mature.
- Be accurate. Do it right the first time.
- Be productive, and do not waste your time or others' time.
- Do what you say you are going to do.

DO YOU HAVE PERSONAL CHALLENGES?

1. Do you think your customers and coworkers face any personal challenges? Of course, they do, and you do too.
2. You have a unique opportunity to brighten their day and yours.
   a) A *sincere* smile and, "It is good to see you," can really help them. But you *must* be sincere!
   b) Be kind. Everyone is fighting their own battles.
   c) Be accurate.
   d) Do not add unnecessary stress to your customer's day, your coworker's day, and your day. Check your personal problems at the entrance door. Pick them up when you leave.
   e) Give your absolute best.

f) Make *everyone* (including your coworkers and supervisor) glad they dealt with you.

g) Be helpful!

TIPS FOR EXCELLENT CUSTOMER SERVICE—VOICE MAIL

1. Speak slowly and clearly when you leave a message; speak upbeat stating your name and organization.
2. Be brief and to the point, but tell them *why* you are calling. This allows them the opportunity to prepare for your conversation.
3. Repeat your phone number and your name at the end of your message.
4. Give them a preferred time to return your call.
5. Say, "Thank you, I will look forward to talking to you soon."
6. Be helpful!

- Be a supportive team player.
- Work harmoniously with your coworkers and supervisors.
- Be receptive to constructive criticism.
- Communicate effectively and courteously.

TIPS FOR EXCELLENT CUSTOMER SERVICE—EMAIL

1. Use the same etiquette as writing a formal letter.
2. If you change the topic of an email thread, change the subject line to reflect the new topic.
3. Try not to begin paragraphs with *I*. Use *you* whenever you can.
4. Start every email with a positive note.
5. Be brief and to the point.
6. Use paragraphs and/or bullet points to make your email more readable.
7. Separate them by thought or point.
8. List your full address and contact information in your signature.
9. Respond promptly, but at least within one business day.
    a) If you cannot, tell them within one business day when you will respond.
10. Be helpful!

TIPS FOR EXCELLENT CUSTOMER SERVICE—TELEPHONE

1. Always speak upbeat. Do not say, "Yes, we can do it, but it is a pain." Do not let your tone of voice convey anything negative.
2. Talk clearly and deliberately. Do *not* sound rushed.
3. Remember, *you* are the organization.
4. Use their name, but not too often.
5. Make them glad they talked with you.
6. Be helpful!

TIPS FOR EXCELLENT CUSTOMER SERVICE—IN-PERSON

1. Follow the same tips for telephone service
2. Smile, but smile sincerely. Show a facial expression that says, "I am glad to see you."
3. Whenever you see, meet, or pass a customer or coworker, acknowledge them. A simple hello is especially important. Do *not* just walk by them. Customers pay your salary, and coworkers are important to your success and the success of your organization! Be courteous and friendly.
4. Use their name, but not too often.
5. When asked, "How are you?" never be negative or complain. Don't say you don't feel well.
6. Be positive! Do not say anything negative about your organization. For example, do not say, "I'd be better if we had more help." Rather, say, "I am fine, thank you. I like working here and helping you." It is vital to say it in a positive and sincere tone. Also, do not say, "I am glad it is

Friday." It sounds like you do not like your job and you would rather not be taking care of your customer.

7. Stay *focused* on your customer. Do *not* talk to coworkers when you are with a customer unless you need their help!
8. Be helpful!

TIPS FOR EXCELLENT CUSTOMER SERVICE—GENERAL

1. Do it right the first time—please be consistently accurate!
2. *Do not talk to or interrupt coworkers unnecessarily*. It may cause them to lose concentration and make an error. Save up questions and ask them together to limit interrupting them often.
3. Know your organization and its history.
4. Improve your communication skills. Learn the following:
    a) How to communicate ideas.
    b) Learn proper grammar.
    c) Do not use profanity.
    d) How to handle a challenging customer.
    e) How to persuade your customers tactfully.
    f) Know what you are going to say in different situations. Perhaps even prepare a script for certain situations. Be ready.

g) Know how to say no, respectfully. Do not be tentative.

h) Do not use jargon or acronyms someone may not understand.

i) If you must interrupt a coworker that is with a customer, always apologize to the customer first.

5. *Always* respond within one business day to phone calls, emails, and correspondence. If you cannot complete the request, let them know within one business day that you will get back to them and give them a timeline.

- Dress appropriately and neatly.
- Follow clean hygiene and personal care.
- Maintain poise in difficult situations.
- Respect everyone and property entrusted to you.
- Be helpful and professional with every customer.
- Continue to improve your knowledge and skills.

Be alert to opportunities to help your customer and, in turn, your organization. Make them *glad* they dealt with you. Be helpful.

WHY SHOULD I CARE ABOUT CUSTOMER SERVICE?

1. It will help you progress, create opportunities, and earn more income.
2. It will make you proud of yourself and your organization. Just imagine the outcome if every one of your coworkers was focused and excellent at customer service.
3. It will create goodwill with your customers and your boss.
4. It will help your organization. Remember, if your organization does well, so will you!

HOW CAN YOU IMPROVE?

1. Educate yourself at work *and* after hours. Invest in your future. Take advantage of the educational opportunities offered by your organization.
2. Stay on top of industry trends and best practices.
3. Welcome negative feedback—*do not get defensive.* Listen objectively.
4. Leave your personal problems at the door. This may be easier said than done, but it is important to your job that you focus on your work. Do not let your personal problems negatively affect your job. If you need help, please seek outside help.

WHAT ELSE CAN YOU DO TO GET AHEAD AT WORK?

1. Follow policies! Your supervisor is busy and challenged. You are an adult. Your supervisor should not have to re-educate you on things you should already know and follow.
2. Follow the chain of command. Always go to your supervisor first. Do not go over your supervisor unless it involves something illegal or unsafe. If you do, realize this is a risky maneuver. Let your conscience decide.
3. Pay attention in meetings and workshops, and do not distract others with unnecessary talking.
4. Know your job so you do not have to ask for help. This includes product knowledge and knowing all policies.
5. Tell your customers and coworkers that you like your job, but tell yourself first. Look for the good about your job. This can be powerful and create a positive atmosphere.

6. Work harmoniously with and support your coworkers and supervisor.
7. Be punctual for work, meetings, and webinars. Your supervisor is busy and should not have to remind you to be on time. Again, you are an adult! Please be on time. Why would you want to create a problem for your supervisor and disrespect your coworkers?
8. Be dependable. Do what you say you are going to do! Damaging your reputation will not help you get ahead.
9. Be helpful and nice to everyone. This is not a difficult practice to improve, and it will help you immensely. Plus, make you happier.
10. Only take *urgent personal calls*, unless you are on break. Remember, you are at work, and you are paid to work not take care of personal business. It also distracts you and cuts into your productivity. If you are on a personal call when your coworkers can hear you, it will distract them too. Taking non-urgent phone calls or messages on organization time will *not* help you progress.
11. Do not chew gum. It can be interpreted as rude.
12. If you are sick, *please* stay home. Customers do not want to deal with you if you are coughing and sneezing. Plus, you do not want to infect

your coworkers. This is also a reminder to save your sick days *for* sick days. You may need them, so do not abuse them. I once had an employee who was sick for ten days one year. Nine of them were on Mondays!

13. Dress appropriately for your job. You only get one chance to make a good first impression. This is common sense. You need to remember that you are presenting yourself to get ahead, and you reflect your organization. You need to be neat and clean. This includes not wearing wrinkled or soiled clothing. You also need to avoid tight or provocative clothing. If you wonder if something is appropriate for work, it probably is not. You are at work, not going out on the town. Please look professional and show pride in yourself.
14. Do not talk too much. Be friendly with everyone, but keep small talk to a minimum. You have work to do. If a customer appears ready to leave, simply say, "Thank you for coming in. Enjoy the rest of your day." Do not extend the conversation by asking a question, especially an open-ended question. This also applies to your coworkers! Do not waste your time and your coworkers' time with unnecessary conversation.

15. Mind your own business. Do not listen to other conversations, and certainly do not inject yourself into the discussion unless you are invited.
16. Do not discuss politics. This is a minefield because each person has their own views, and those views may be strong. No matter how convinced you are in your own belief, others may feel just the opposite. It is best not to engage in politics with customers and coworkers. Please stay neutral at work.
17. Be a team player. People will notice.
18. Volunteer when your supervisor asks for help, even if you would rather not. It will help you get ahead.
19. Show pride in your workplace. For example, if you see a piece of trash on the floor or in the parking lot, pick it up and dispose of it. If there are dirty dishes in the sink, wash them.
20. Give management the benefit of the doubt. Even if your employer communicates very well, it is not always practical to share all the information behind a decision.
21. Sincerely say, "Please and thank you" often.

22. Catch your co-workers doing something well and complement them for it.
23. Pay attention to how other business employees treat you. Jot the experiences down for reference, and share them with your supervisor. Emulate them if you are pleased with their service. Learn from poor service so you do not repeat it yourself.

• Know and follow the chain of command. • Give management the benefit of the doubt. • Know and fulfill your job description duties efficiently. • Know your employer's policies.

This is not nuclear physics!

— *Take pride in yourself and your organization!*
— *Use a positive and upbeat tone with everyone.*
— Do *not* be moody or short with anyone.
— Be good at what you do.
— Show enthusiasm in all that you do.

- — Make everyone glad they interacted with you.
- — Be helpful with everyone.

Things will not happen overnight. But you will see results, not just for you but for your coworkers too. Be upbeat and positive. It may take months to see results, but you will see a change and feel better about yourself

Set your goals, develop your plan, and most importantly, be patient and persistent in your efforts. If you want to make more money, you must earn it. Start right now!

You will be happier—so will your organization!

Never stop improving. Make this process a habit, and you will see significant progress in pay and personal satisfaction. No one else will do it for you.

Make it work!

WHAT STORIES DO YOU HAVE ABOUT GREAT CUSTOMER SERVICE OR POOR CUSTOMER SERVICE?

Here are some of my stories:

1. I had an appointment to have my tires rotated. On my way to the appointment, I noticed that I was due for an oil change. When I arrived, I asked if they would have time to change my oil. The rep said, very abruptly, "Nope, not with what I have going today."

   I understand I did not have an appointment for an oil change, but he could have handled this so much better. He could have used a friendlier tone and said, "I am sorry, but I have a full schedule today. Would you like to make an appointment now so we can take care of it for you?"

He never asked to make an appointment to fulfill my needs. He turned me off and lost an oil change—and a customer.

2. I was at a lumberyard getting lumber. I asked the young man helping me how his day was going. He said, "It would be better if I had more help." No matter how upset you may be, this comment is counterproductive. First, complaining to a customer accomplishes nothing. In fact, it turned me off and created a negative image of his company. This is not what his employer wants him to do, and it did nothing to solve the problem.

3. I walked up to a checkout lane, and the clerk rather abruptly said, "I am closed. I am closed." Why not say, "I am sorry, sir, I just closed my lane. Would you mind using another lane?"

4. My brother wanted to purchase a gun safe, and the sales representative was courteous but did not smile once. My brother needed a cart, so the rep told him he (my brother) could get one in the front of the store. My brother walked from the back of the store to the front only to be told

the type of cart he needed was in the back corner of the store. It was closer to the gun safe than the front of the store! This sales representative, if he wanted to be helpful, could have simply said, "I will get a cart for you, just stay here, and I will be back right away." First, he never smiled. Second, he was not helpful.

5. My wife called a car mechanic to make an appointment and explained her problem. His response, "Well we can do it, but it is a real pain." Why would he say this? He should have just said, "Yes, we can take care of that for you."

6. A good friend of mine had a bolt in his tire, so he visited a tire store. The service representative told him he could check out tires online and order them. Then they would install it for him. He went to a different source for his tire! If the first rep had done her job and been helpful by ordering the tire for him, she would not have lost a sale.

7. I was sitting at a bar having a typical Wisconsin Friday fish fry at a local tavern. The cook came out of the kitchen door criticizing the bar-

tender for making a mistake. She did it in a loud, angry, and reprimanding tone embarrassing the bartender, herself, and the many patrons present. This is inexcusable and totally wrong. She showed lack of empathy, lack of poise, and alienated her coworker and the patrons. Always criticize someone in private. Praise them in public.

Please share your own stories with me by emailing me at seasonedhelp@gmail.com. Thanks.

List your own stories here, and use them to improve your customer service.

APPENDIX A

To satisfy employers with high standards, you should:

1. Be dependable.
2. Be honest and ethical.
3. Be responsible and mature.
4. Be accurate. Do it right the first time.
5. Be productive, and do not waste your time or others' time.
6. Be punctual.
7. Do what you say you are going to do.
8. Be friendly and helpful to *everyone.*
9. Be a supportive team player.
10. Work harmoniously with your coworkers and supervisors.
11. Be receptive to constructive criticism.
12. Communicate effectively and courteously.
13. Dress appropriately and neatly.
14. Follow clean hygiene and personal care.
15. Maintain poise in difficult situations.

16. Respect everyone and the property entrusted to you.
17. Be helpful and professional with every customer.
18. Continue to improve your knowledge and skills.
19. Know and follow the chain of command.
20. Give management the benefit of the doubt.
21. Know and fulfill your job description duties efficiently.
22. Know your employer's policies.
23. Thoroughly know your employer's products and services that relate to you directly.
24. Be aware of your employer's other products and services, in general.
25. Promote your employer, and be loyal.
26. If you need help, please ask!
27. Criticize in private. Praise in public.

APPENDIX B

A: What is the *first* thing I am going to do to increase my value to my employer and take pride in myself?

____

____

____

My three steps to accomplish it:

1.

2.

3.

I will accomplish this goal no later than ____________.

List how accomplishing this goal will help you and your employer.

B: Here is the *second* thing I will do:

____

____

____

My three steps to accomplish it:

1.

2.

3.

I will accomplish this goal no later than ___________.

List how accomplishing this goal will help you and your employer.

____

____

____

C: Here is the *third* thing I will do:

____

____

____

My three steps to accomplish it:

1.

2.

3.

I will accomplish this goal no later than ____________.

List how accomplishing this goal will help you and your employer.

____

____

____

You get the idea. Once you have completed these three goals, list the next three, and continue your path to become more valuable.

NOTES

NOTES

ABOUT THE AUTHOR

Thomas "Tom" C. Pinnow earned a BBA from the University of Wisconsin-Eau Claire in business management. He worked two years at a finance company, including managing a branch office, sold life insurance for five years, worked in banking as a vice president and senior loan officer, and then spent over twenty-seven years as the president of a small credit union. He is a graduate of the American Bankers Association Commercial Lending program and is a Credit Union Development Educator (CUDE). He also served in leadership roles in several community organizations, from high school to the present. Member service has always been a priority for him, so he wanted to share his observations and experience from his forty-plus years in management to help you increase your value and earn more money.

Tom lives in Deerfield, Wisconsin, and can be reached at seasonedhelp@gmail.com.

www.ingramcontent.com/pod-product-compliance
Lightning Source LLC
Chambersburg PA
CBHW031002180726
47993CB00018B/1522

* 9 7 9 8 8 8 6 1 6 3 9 6 4 *